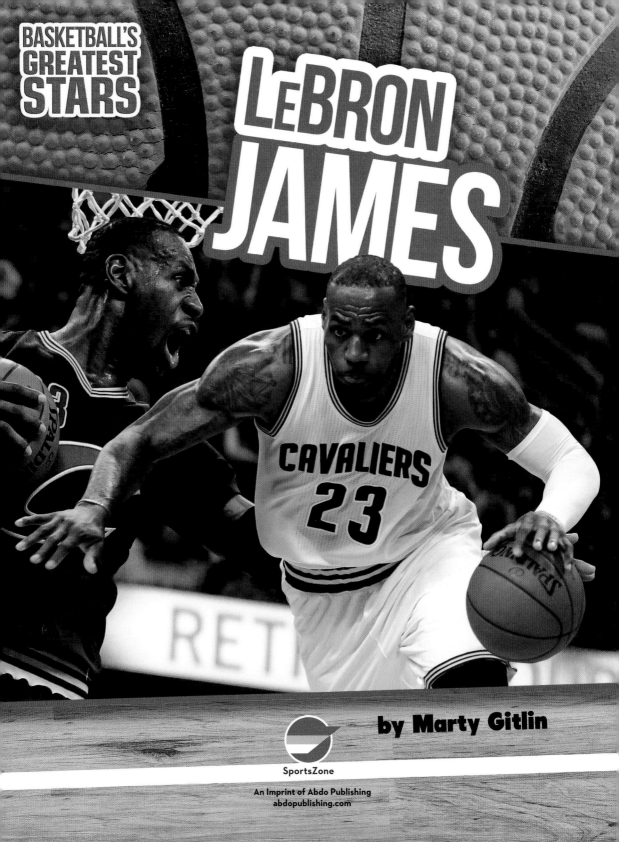

BASKETBALL'S GREATEST STARS

LeBRON JAMES

by Marty Gitlin

SportsZone

An Imprint of Abdo Publishing
abdopublishing.com

abdopublishing.com

Published by Abdo Publishing, a division of ABDO, PO Box 398166, Minneapolis, Minnesota 55439. Copyright © 2017 by Abdo Consulting Group, Inc. International copyrights reserved in all countries. No part of this book may be reproduced in any form without written permission from the publisher. SportsZone™ is a trademark and logo of Abdo Publishing.

Printed in the United States of America, North Mankato, Minnesota
102016
012017

THIS BOOK CONTAINS
RECYCLED MATERIALS

Cover Photos: Tony Dejak/AP Images, foreground, background
Interior Photos: Tony Dejak/AP Images, 1 (foreground), 1 (background), 16-17, 26-27; Marcio Jose Sanchez/AP Images, 4-5, 8-9; Eric Risberg/AP Images, 6, 7; Seth Poppel/Yearbook Library, 10, 11, 14; Bruce Schwartzman/AP Images, 12-13, 15; Michael Conroy/AP Images, 18; Duane Burleson/AP Images, 19; Eric Gay/AP Images, 20-21; J. Pat Carter/AP Images, 22-23; David Richard/AP Images, 24; Lynne Sladky/AP Images, 25; Ben Margot/AP Images, 28; Kathy Willens/AP Images, 29

Editor: Todd Kortemeier
Series Designer: Laura Polzin

Publisher's Cataloging-in-Publication Data
Names: Gitlin, Marty, author.
Title: LeBron James / by Marty Gitlin.
Description: Minneapolis, MN : Abdo Publishing, 2017. | Series: Basketball's
    greatest stars | Includes index.
Identifiers: LCCN 2016945487 | ISBN 9781680785470 (lib. bdg.) |
    ISBN 9781680798104 (ebook)
Subjects: LCSH: James, LeBron, 1984- --Juvenile literature. | Basketball players--
    United States--Biography--Juvenile literature.
Classification: DDC 796.323 [B]--dc23
LC record available at http://lccn.loc.gov/2016945487

CONTENTS

CLEVELAND HERO

It was the biggest game in Cleveland Cavaliers history. Cavs fans had never seen a championship. And their hero was about to do something amazing.

The date was June 19, 2016. The team that had never won a National Basketball Association (NBA) title was playing in Game 7 of the finals in Oakland against the Golden State Warriors. The game was tied 89-89 with less than two minutes remaining.

LeBron James, *center*, drives to the hoop in Game 7 of the 2016 NBA Finals.

Suddenly the Warriors were on a fast break. Forward Andre Iguodala streaked to the basket for what looked like an easy layup. But Cavaliers superstar LeBron James came out of nowhere.

He leaped high into the air and blocked the shot. Time was running out, and James had saved his team from falling behind.

James led the Cavaliers in scoring with 27 points in Game 7.

James, 23, blocks Andre Iguodala's shot late in the 4th quarter to keep the game tied.

FAST FACT

James was named Most Valuable Player (MVP) of the finals. He was the first player in finals history to lead both teams in points, rebounds, assists, steals, and blocks.

Teammate Kyrie Irving then nailed a three-point shot with under a minute to go. The Cavaliers held on to win their first championship. Fans back home went crazy. It was the first title for any Cleveland sports team in 52 years.

James embraced his teammates. His emotions took over. He dropped to his knees and cried for joy. He had promised to deliver Cleveland a crown. And he had kept that promise.

James, *center*, gets emotional celebrating the championship with his teammates.

FAST FACT

The city of Cleveland threw an incredible party after the Cavaliers won the title. More than 1 million fans attended the event downtown.

GROWING INTO GREATNESS

LeBron James was born in Akron, Ohio, on December 30, 1984. His mother was just 16 when he was born, and she raised him on her own. LeBron never knew his father.

LeBron grew up poor. He and his mother moved a lot and he missed almost 100 school days in fourth grade. Two men soon changed his life. One was football coach Bruce Kelker. In 1993, when LeBron was eight years old, Kelker invited him to join his team. Football was LeBron's favorite sport. He became a young football standout. He continued to star in that sport in high school.

LeBron didn't start playing any sports until he was eight.

Before he became known for wearing 23, LeBron wore number 32 in honor of superstar Julius "Dr. J" Erving.

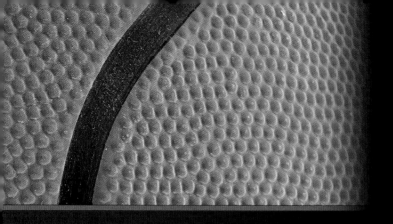

Another positive influence was his youth basketball coach, Frankie Walker. Late in fourth grade, LeBron and his mother had to move. Walker offered to take LeBron in so that he could stay in school. The next year, he went to school every day and improved his grades.

LeBron's life turned around. He went on to play basketball at St. Vincent-St. Mary High School. His talent made the entire country take notice.

LeBron was widely considered the best high school player in the country.

FAST FACT

LeBron led
St. Vincent-St. Mary to
three state titles in four
years. He twice scored
50 or more points in
a game during his
senior season.

LeBron won the state tournament MVP award as a freshman. He was named Mr. Basketball in Ohio the next three years. He became such a sensation that *Sports Illustrated* placed him on its cover in 2002.

LeBron was already a superstar. But he was just getting started.

LeBron won the Gatorade National Player of the Year award as a junior, the first player to do so.

LeBron was such a star in high school that ESPN televised some of his games nationally.

FAST FACT

In 2013 James donated $1 million to renovate St. Vincent-St. Mary's gym. He felt that the school had given him so much that he wanted to give back.

THE NBA'S NEW KING

LeBron James did not have to go far to begin his NBA career. Cleveland took him with the first pick in the 2003 draft. He'd be playing just a short drive from his hometown.

The Cavaliers won only 17 games in 2002-03. They needed help. And James was amazing from the start. He was a brilliant passer. He dribbled and scored with strength. He could make shots from the outside. And he worked hard on defense.

FAST FACT

James enjoyed the best rookie year ever for a player coming right out of high school. He averaged 20.9 points per game and was named Rookie of the Year.

James was thrilled to be drafted by his hometown Cleveland Cavaliers.

The Cavaliers continued to improve after James arrived. They finally blossomed in 2007. They played the Detroit Pistons for a chance to go to the NBA Finals. Game 5 was very close. James was on fire. He scored 29 of Cleveland's last 30 points. And he was far from finished.

Detroit led 107-104 with about a minute left. James came to the rescue. He heaved a 25-foot jumper that hit nothing but net. The game was tied. Seconds later he burst through the Detroit defense. He was too strong to stop. He scored the game-winning layup.

James played with Team USA at the 2004 Summer Olympics and won a bronze medal.

James scores the winning basket in Game 5 of the 2007 Eastern Conference finals.

The Cavaliers also won Game 6 to make it to the NBA Finals for the first time. And it was James who made it possible. He was already the greatest player in team history. He led the league in scoring in 2008. He won MVP in 2009 and 2010.

But he wasn't able to win a championship for Cleveland. The man nicknamed "King James" decided he needed to play where he had a better chance of winning a title.

James averaged 22 points per game in the 2007 NBA Finals, but the Cavs were swept by the San Antonio Spurs.

FAST FACT

The Cavaliers finished with the best record in the NBA in 2009 and 2010. But they were knocked out of the playoffs before they could reach the finals.

FEELING THE HEAT

The world wanted to know where LeBron James was going. His decision was televised on ESPN. He announced that he was heading to Miami to play for the Heat.

James explained later why he left Cleveland. He said he was like a college kid yearning to leave home and explore a new world. In 2012 and 2013 he was incredible in leading Miami to NBA titles. In 2012 his team was on the brink of elimination. But he exploded for 45 points and 15 rebounds in Boston to save the season.

James, *right*, is introduced as a member of the Miami Heat along with new teammates Chris Bosh, *left*, and Dwyane Wade, *center*.

FAST FACT

James married his high school sweetheart Savannah in September 2013. They have three children together.

James averaged 27 points per game in his four seasons with the Heat. Many people now believed he was the greatest player ever.

But something was missing in his basketball life. He still had not won a championship for Cleveland. The world waited eagerly for another decision. And in July 2014, he announced that he was returning to the Cavaliers. James was going home.

James celebrates with the championship trophy that had eluded him in Cleveland.

HOME SWEET HOME

For Cleveland, losing LeBron James meant losing many games. And his return resulted in many victories.

The Cavaliers spent four years struggling while James was gone. He came back to turn them into winners. He had matured as a player. He was still an incredible scorer. But he also worked to make his teammates better. He was now considered one of the greatest passers in NBA history.

FAST FACT

James teamed up with another top draft pick in his return to Cleveland. Point guard Kyrie Irving was taken first overall in 2011.

Fans in Cleveland were thrilled when James announced he was returning home to play for the Cavaliers.

No Cleveland sports team had won a title since 1964. The fans were desperate to celebrate one. James wanted to celebrate with them. That dream was close to turning into a reality in 2015. He led the Cavaliers back into the NBA Finals. But injuries to Irving and forward Kevin Love doomed Cleveland. They lost to Golden State in six games.

James vowed to avenge that defeat and win a crown for Cleveland. And a year later, he did just that. James showed that he was still at the top of his game.

James led the Cavaliers to the NBA Finals in his first season back with the team.

James goes up for a reverse dunk at the 2015 NBA All-Star Game.

TIMELINE

1984
LeBron James is born on December 30 in Akron, Ohio.

2002
James is featured on the cover of *Sports Illustrated*.

2003
St. Vincent-St. Mary High School wins its third state title in four years with the help of 25 points from James.

2003
The Cavaliers select James with the first pick in the NBA Draft on June 26.

2007
James scores 48 points in a playoff win in Detroit to help Cleveland reach its first NBA Finals.

2010
James announces on national television that he is joining the Miami Heat.

2013
Miami wins its second straight NBA crown on June 20.

2014
James announces that he is returning to the Cavaliers.

2016
James leads the Cavaliers to their first NBA championship.

GLOSSARY

ASSIST
A pass that leads directly to a scored basket.

FAST BREAK
When one team moves the ball up the court quickly.

LAYUP
A shot made from close to the basket; an easy shot.

PLAYOFFS
A set of games played after the regular season that decides which team will be the champion.

REBOUND
Grabbing a missed shot in basketball.

RENOVATE
To improve the physical conditions of a building.

ROOKIE
A first-year player.

SWEPT
When a team loses every game in a series.

INDEX

ABOUT THE AUTHOR

Marty Gitlin is a freelance sportswriter and author based in Cleveland. He has had more than 100 books published since 2006 and won more than 45 awards as a journalist.

9